The Nature Kid's Guide to SEALS

DAVID ANDERSON

LP Media Inc. Publishing
Text copyright © 2026 by LP Media Inc.
All rights reserved.

For information address LP Media Inc. Publishing,
30012 Variolite St NW, Princeton MN 55371
www.lpmedia.org

Publication Data

Seals
The Nature Kid's Guide to Seals — First edition.

Summary: "Learn all about Seals, the Nature Kid Way"
— Provided by publisher.

ISBN: 979-8-89818-156-7

[1. Seals – Non-Fiction] I. Title.

Title: The Nature Kid's Guide to Seals

CONTENTS

CHILLY COASTS

Splash! A seal dives down into icy water. Its big eyes look around for fish.

Seals live in cold places around the world. They spend time both in the ocean and on land. Rocky shores and icy beaches are their homes.

These animals love chilly coasts because cold water has lots of fish to eat. When they are not swimming, seals rest on rocks, ice, and sandy beaches.

Some seals live near the North Pole. Others live near the South Pole. Harbor seals live along both the east and west coasts of North America.

Every type of seal picks a home that fits its needs.

SEAL SPOTS

Bark! A gray seal rests on a Scottish shore. Its wet fur shines in the sun.

Seals live on every continent. They even live in Africa! They swim in oceans all across the world.

Harp seals live in the Arctic Ocean. Leopard seals hunt in Antarctic waters. Elephant seals swim near California.

Mediterranean monk seals live in warm seas. They swim near Greece. Weddell seals stay close to Antarctica all year.

Hawaiian monk seals only live near Hawaii. Only about 1,600 of them are left today.

SUPER
SIZED

Thump! A huge elephant seal lands on the sandy beach.

Seals come in many sizes. Some are small. Others are giants!

Southern elephant seals are the biggest. Males can weigh up to 8,800 pounds and grow 20 feet long. That is heavier and longer than a car!

Ringed seals are the smallest. They weigh only about 150 pounds and grow to just 5 feet long. That is a big difference from their giant cousins!

A male elephant seal can be ten times heavier than a female elephant seal.

FLIPPERS FIRST

Swoosh! A seal glides through the water. Its flippers push it forward.

Seals have four flippers. Two are in front and two are in back. These flippers help seals swim fast and steer through the water.

The front flippers help the seal steer and change direction. Back flippers push the seal forward like a boat motor.

On land, seals move differently. They wiggle and bounce on their bellies. Their flippers are not made for walking, which is why seals look clumsy on rocks and beaches.

WHISKER
WONDERS

Snap! A harbor seal looks around. It's whiskers are it's secret weapon!

Seals have great whiskers. Scientists call them **vibrissae**. The whiskers can feel tiny moves in the water.

When a fish swims past. It leaves a trail of movement in the water. A seal's whiskers feel this trail. They work even in the dark!

Seals hear well under water. Their big eyes help too. They can even see in dark, cloudy water.

Each whisker has over 1,000 nerve endings. They are like tiny fish detectors!

BLUBBER ARMOR

Whoosh! A harp seal pup dives into freezing water. But its body stays warm inside.

Seals have a thick layer of fat called **blubber**. Some seals have blubber up to 4 inches thick!

Blubber keeps seals warm in icy oceans. It works like a cozy blanket wrapped around their whole body.

Blubber also helps seals float. The fat is lighter than water. This makes swimming easier and saves energy during long dives.

Blubber stores energy too. Seals can live off their fat when food is hard to find.

FISH FEAST

Chomp! A harbor seal catches a slippery fish. It gulps the meal down fast.

Seals eat many kinds of fish. They love herring, cod, and salmon. Some seals eat over 30 pounds of fish each day!

Seals do not chew their food. They swallow fish whole or in big chunks. Their sharp teeth help them grip slippery prey first.

Seals also eat squid, octopus, and shrimp. The foods they eat depend on where they live.

Leopard seals will hunt penguins and even other seals too!

17

DIVE DEEP

Glub! A seal slips beneath the waves. Down it goes!

Seals are expert divers. They hunt for food deep in the ocean. Some dive over 1,000 feet down!

Before a deep dive, seals slow their heartbeat. This helps them save oxygen. Their bodies also store extra oxygen in their blood.

Elephant seals are the best divers. They can stay underwater for up to 2 hours! Common seals usually dive for 3 to 10 minutes.

Seals chase fish through dark, cold water. They twist and turn fast to catch their prey.

Weddell seals dive under Antarctic ice. They can reach depths of 2,000 feet!

DANGER LURKS

Swoosh! A great white shark circles nearby. A seal darts away fast.

Seals face danger from many predators. Great white sharks hunt seals near rocky shores. Orcas also chase seals in cold waters.

On land, polar bears hunt seals in the Arctic. They wait by breathing holes in the ice. When a seal comes up for air, the bear strikes.

Leopard seals hunt smaller seals in Antarctica. These fierce hunters use sharp teeth to catch their prey.

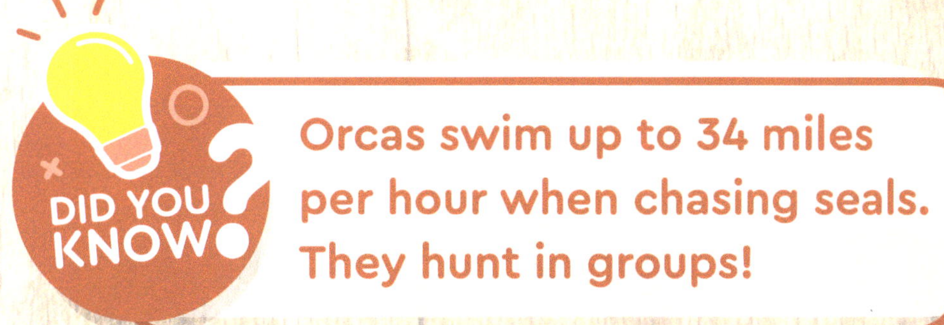

SLIP AWAY

22

Zoom! A seal rockets through the water. It escapes!

Seals have many ways to stay safe. Speed is their best trick. They can swim up to 23 miles per hour!

In the water, seals zigzag to confuse predators. They make sharp turns that sharks cannot follow.

Since they move so slowly on land, seals stay near the water's edge. If danger comes, they slide quickly into the sea.

Seals swim much faster than even Olympic swimmers. The fastest human only swims about 5 miles per hour!

FLOP WALK

Flop! A seal lands on the beach. It wiggles forward on its belly!

Seals are graceful in the water. On land? Not so much! True seals cannot walk. Their back flippers do not bend forward like legs.

Instead, seals bounce and wiggle on their bellies. They scrunch up like caterpillars and push forward. It looks silly, but it works!

Some seals can move across ice and sand surprisingly fast this way

Elephant seals can wiggle up to 3 miles inland to find the perfect resting spot on the beach!

HALF ASLEEP

Zzz! A seal floats at the surface. It's asleep, but only half its brain is resting!

Seals have amazing ways to sleep. Some float at the surface like a bobbing bottle. Others sink to the ocean floor and nap there!

Seals can shut down half their brain while the other half stays awake. This helps them watch for danger while they rest.

When sleeping underwater, they hold their breath and pop up to breathe without fully waking up.

Scientists call a floating, sleeping seal a "bottling" seal because it bobs upright in the water like a bottle!

COLONY
CREW

Honk! Many seals crowd a rocky beach. They rest in a big group.

Seals live in big groups. These groups are called **colonies**. Some colonies have thousands of seals!

They crowd together on beaches, rocks, and ice. Seals rest side by side, sometimes even piled on top of each other.

In the water, a group of seals is called a **pod**. Pods swim and hunt for fish together.

Some seal colonies are very noisy. Their loud calls can be heard from over a mile away!

BARKING BOYS

Bark! A male elephant seal bellows loudly. He wants to be heard!

Male seals make loud calls during mating season. Male Northern elephant seals have roars that reach up to 131 **decibels**. These deep bellows can be heard up to 5 miles away!

Males often fight each other. They push, bite, and slam their bodies together. The strongest males win these battles.

Females pick a new male each year, so males must keep fighting to prove they are the best.

Male elephant seals can go without eating for up to 3 months during mating season!

PUFFY PUPS

Squeak! A fluffy white harp seal pup calls for its mom on the icy shore.

Baby seals are called pups. Many are born with soft, white fur. This fluffy coat keeps them warm on cold ice and beaches.

Seal pups grow very fast. Harp seal pups gain about 5 pounds every day! This is because their mother's milk is very rich and fatty.

Pups cannot swim at first. Instead, they stay on land while their bodies grow stronger. After a few weeks, they learn to dive and catch food.

Ringed seal pups are born in snow dens! Mother seals dig caves in the snow to keep their babies hidden and safe.

MOM KNOWS

DID YOU KNOW?
Weddell seal moms teach pups to swim in icy Antarctic waters.

Snort! A mother seal nuzzles her pup. She knows her baby's smell.

Each seal pup has a special smell. Moms learn this scent right after birth.

Mothers also know their pup's voice. A pup's call sounds different from all others. This helps moms find their baby in a crowded group. Antarctic fur seal mothers can recognize their pup's call from up to 209 feet away!

Many seal mothers stay close to their pups for weeks. But hooded seal mothers nurse for only 3 to 5 days. This is the shortest nursing time of any mammal. But their milk is so rich and fatty that the pup gains about 15 pounds a day and doubles its size before mom leaves!

MELTING ICE

Crack! A chunk of ice breaks off. A seal pup watches it float away.

Sea ice is melting faster than ever before. Many seals need ice to rest and have pups. Without it, they must swim farther to find safe spots.

Ringed seals dig dens in snow on ice. When ice melts early, pups lose their homes.

Scientists are studying seals to learn how warming oceans affect them.

Arctic ice has shrunk so much that some seals now swim hundreds of miles to find places to rest and hunt!

SAVING
SEALS

Chirp! A scientist watches a seal come up onto the beach. He's taking notes.

People work hard to protect seals. Scientists count seals and track where they swim. This helps us learn what seals need to survive.

Many beaches have rules to keep seals safe. Visitors must stay far away from resting seals.

Rescue groups help sick or hurt seals. They nurse them back to health. Then they release them into the ocean.

Rescued seal pups sometimes drink fish smoothies until they learn to eat whole fish!

GLOSSARY

vibrissae

The special whiskers on a seal's face that help it feel things in the water.

blubber

A thick layer of fat under a seal's skin that keeps it warm.

colonies

Big groups of seals that live and rest together.

pod

A group of seals who are in the water.

decibels

A way to measure how loud a sound is